Fourteen Songs, Two Weddings and a Funeral

Based on Rajshri Productions' film Hum Aapke Hain Koun

Adapted for the stage by
Sudha Bhuchar *and* **Kristine Landon-Smith**

Methuen Drama

Methuen

3 5 7 9 10 8 6 4 2

First published in Great Britain in 2001 by Methuen Publishing Limited
215 Vauxhall Bridge Road, London SW1V 1EJ

Methuen Publishing Limited Reg. No. 3543167

A CIP catalogue record is available from the British Library

ISBN 0 413 76480 X

Typeset by SX Composing DTP, Rayleigh, Essex
Printed and bound in Great Britain by
Cox & Wyman Ltd, Reading, Berkshire

Tamasha Theatre Company
with the Birmingham Repertory Theatre
and the Lyric Theatre Hammersmith
present:

Fourteen Songs,
Two Weddings
and a Funeral

Adapted from Rajshri Productions'
Hum Aapke Hain Koun
by Sudha Bhuchar and Kristine Landon-Smith

First performance of this production,
Wednesday 19th September 2001

This play was first performed in the studio at the Lyric Theatre Hammersmith, Wednesday 11th November 1998 with the following cast members:

Lalloo	Rajesh Bedi
Arun/Dilip/Doctor	Ajay Chhabra
Pooja/Rita	Meneka Das
Kaka/Gautam	Shiv Grewal
Rajesh	Raza Jaffrey
Bhagwanti/Radha	Shobu Kapoor
Prem	Pravesh Kumar
Nisha	Parminder Nagra
Professor/Karan	Rehan Sheikh
Kamla/Nandini	Sameena Zehra

This production was originally supported by

Barclays stage *partners*

with THE **ARTS COUNCIL** OF ENGLAND

Tamasha wishes to thank
Clickwalla.com, Anand Shah, Mr. G. K. Noon,
North Middlesex Hospice Estates, Outcaste Records,
Firechaser, Sullivan Colour Lab, Ruby Rajah
Clear Cut Pictures and Shammi Aulakh

CAST
(in order of appearance)

Prem	Pushpinder Chani
Nisha	Mala Ghedia
Lalloo	Dinesh Shukla
Bhagwanti	Shobu Kapoor
	Sudha Bhuchar
Arun	Ajay Chhabra
Kaka	Lyndam Gregory
Rajesh	Anand Chulani
Pooja	Meera Kumar
Kamla	Pooja Ghai
Professor	Shiv Grewal
Dancer/company	Melody Woodhead
Dancer/company	Rachel Tanh
Dancer/company	Sara Leone
Dancer/company	Melissa Hunte

All musical numbers sung by the original cast
All other parts are played by members of the company

Director	Kristine Landon-Smith
Designer	Sue Mayes
Lighting Designer	Chris Davey
Musical Arrangements	Barrie Bignold
Sound Design	Mike Furness
Sound Operator	Nick Manning
Song Lyrics	Shaun McCarthy
	and Felix Cross
Choreographers	Sneha Mistri
	and Kristine Landon-Smith
Dance Tutor	Indiana Seivright
Project Manager	Kathy Bourne
Project Assistant	Debra Clarke
Production Manager	Dennis Charles
Company Manager	Lisa Buckley
Deputy Stage Manager	Ros Terry
Assistant Stage Manager	Thaddius Moustrides
Costume Supervisor	Bushy Westfallen
Wardrobe Mistress	Miriam Ellis

The Company

Sudha Bhuchar (Adaptor & Bhagwanti)
Sudha is co-founder of Tamasha Theatre Company. She is both an actor and a playwright. Her many acting credits include: *EastEnders* (BBC); *The Archers* (BBC Radio) and *Haroun and the Sea of Stories* (Royal National Theatre). Her writing credits for Tamasha include: *Untouchable*, *A Tainted Dawn* and *Balti Kings*. She also writes regularly for BBC Radio drama.

Barrie Bignold (Musical Arrangements)
Barrie's music for television includes: *The Shop*, *The Builders*, *Burgled* (all BBC), *Time Team* and the acclaimed documentary *Road Raj* (for Channel 4). His composing work traverses all aspects of the media and his many theatre scores have included *Peter Pan* (Chichester Festival), *Twelfth Night* (British Actors' Shakespeare Company) and Tamasha's *Balti Kings*.

Pushpinder Chani (Prem)
A graduate from Birmingham's School of Speech and Drama, Pushpinder's recent theatre work includes: *Skeletons*, *Blissful Ignorance* and *The Party* (Birmingham Rep), *Flying Colours* (Greenwich Theatre) and *Monkey Magic* (Midlands Arts Centre). He recently made his TV debut in *Brum*.

Ajay Chhabra (Arun)
Ajay performed in Tamasha's first production, *Untouchable*, and was also a member of the original cast for *Fourteen Songs*. His many theatre credits include: *Indian Ink* (Aldwych), *Arrange That Marriage*, *Helmet* (Traverse) and *Bollywood 2000* (Riverside Studios). Film and TV credits include: *The Bill*, *Casualty* (BBC) and *Roots* (Channel 4). Ajay has also directed several award-winning productions and is Artistic Director of the East London Mela.

Anand Chulani (Rajesh)
Anand has played a variety of classical roles with Georgetown Classical Theater, DC and has enjoyed regular sessions as a stand up comic in Los Angeles and New York. Recently he has filmed a pilot for stand up comedy for Channel Five, and has appeared in various television and film works, including *Spoof!* and *American Chai*.

Chris Davey (Lighting Designer)
Chris's theatre designs include *The Three Sisters* (Oxford Stage Company); *Shining Souls* (Peter Hall Season at the Old Vic); *In a Little World of our Own* and *Endgame* (Donmar Warehouse); *The Colour of Justice* (Tricycle Theatre) and *Balti Kings* (Tamasha Theatre Company). Dance theatre credits include *Transatlantic Tap* (Dance Umbrella) and *Turn of the Tide* (Shobana Jeyasingh Dance Company). Opera credits include *Gli Equivoci Nei Sembiante* (Batignano Opera Festival), *The Picture of Dorian Gray* (Opera de Monte Carlo) and *Faust* (Surrey Opera).

Mike Furness (Sound Design)
This is Mike's sixth sound design for Tamasha, having also designed for companies such as Paines Plough, the Tricycle Theatre and the Edinburgh and Brighton Festivals. Other designs include several shows for the RSC and the West End. Mike produces talking books and is also a consultant for Cameron Mackintosh Consultants.

Pooja Ghai (Kamla)
Trained at the London Academy of Performing Arts, this is Pooja's first role with Tamasha. Other theatre credits include *A Midsummer Night's Dream* (The Man in the Moon), *Unsung Lullaby* (Finborough Theatre), *Heroes* (Blue Elephant Theatre), and *Tales from the Vienna Woods* (The Gate Theatre).

Mala Ghedia (Nisha)
Brought up in Australia, Mala is a recent graduate of the Webber Douglas School in London. Her television credits to date include: *Home and Away* and a presenter and reporter for *MTN News* in Australia. This is Mala's first production with Tamasha. Mala is dedicating her performance to her parents, Prem and Damyanti.

Lyndam Gregory (Kaka)
A graduate of Webber Douglas, Lyndam has appeared in countless television series' including, *EastEnders*, *Surgical Spirit*s, *London's Burning* and *Doctors*. Theatre work includes Kali Theatre's *River On Fire*, the Sanskrit classic *Shakuntala's Ring* and more recently, Andy in the critically acclaimed *Woman In Mind* at the Bolton Octagon. Lyndam also has considerable radio experience, his many roles including Bharat in Radio 4's Ramayana.

Shiv Grewal (Professor)
Shiv has worked with Tamasha on four other productions and is returning to this show from the original cast. His many television appearances include: *The Liver Birds*, *2.4 Children*, *Family Pride*, *The Bill* and *In a Land of Plenty*. His most recent theatre work includes Tamasha's *Balti Kings* and *Baywatch Cymru* for the Sherman Theatre. Extensive radio credits include BBC's *The Archers*.

Melissa Hunte (Dancer)
Melissa trained at Lewisham College and London Studio Centre and is both a dancer and a choreographer. Her professional stage appearances include *Recall* (National Tour and The Royal Opera House - Darshan Singh Bhullar) and *The King and I* (European Tour). Melissa has also danced in numerous music videos including videos for Lionel Richie, U2, Craig David and Melanie B as well as appearing in a variety of TV commercials. Melissa would like to thank her family and friends for supporting her over the years.

Shobu Kapoor (Bhagwanti)
Shobu trained at Drama Studio London and has an MA in Literary Honours from Bombay University. Theatre credits include: *Danton's Death* (Tara Arts); *Nae Problem* (7:84 Theatre Company); *A Night In Tunisia* (Theatre Royal Stratford East). This is her 4th production with Tamasha having performed in *House of the Sun* and also *Women of the Dust* and the original *Fourteen Songs*... Television credits include: *EastEnders* as Gita Kapoor (regular character) and Nasreen in *Family Pride*.

Meera Kumar (Pooja)

Meera trained at the City Lit. Theatre work includes the award-winning *Bullets Through the Golden Stream*, for which Meera won the best actress award in the UK Asian Drama Fringe Festival, for her 3-generation role performance. TV credits include *The Bill* and a variety of Children's BBC comedy. Film work includes *The Fifth Element* and working with Hollywood Director Roger Corman, as Mother Nature on Greenpeace's *Children*. A keen fire-twirler, Meera undertook film and television roles whilst living in Australia and Japan.

Kristine Landon-Smith (Director)

Kristine is joint founder and Artistic Director of Tamasha and has also directed all of the company's shows. Other companies she has worked with include the Royal Court Theatre, Hull Truck Company and she has been an Associate Director of the Bristol Old Vic. Her 1996 production, *East is East*, was nominated for an Olivier award and the original production of *Fourteen Songs* won the Barclays Theatre Award for Best New Musical. Kristine produces regularly for BBC radio.

Sara Leone (Dancer)

Born in Italy and trained in both Rome and Milan, Sara has worked extensively as an actor, dancer and singer both abroad and in the UK. Recent credits include: *Swing* (Riverside Sudios), *In Our Time* (Palladium) and *White Folks* (Tricycle).

Sue Mayes (Designer)

Sue has designed all of Tamasha's shows. Her career started with residencies at Ipswich Rep, the Belgrade Theatre and the Liverpool Everyman and her other free-lance work has included designs for Talawa Theatre Company, Bristol Old Vic, Theatre Royal Stratford East and the Southwark Playhouse.

Dinesh Shukla (Lalloo)

Dinesh, opted out of the 'Rat Race' 6 years ago to pursue a career in IT, where he is enjoying continued success. Prior to this period, his professional acting career spanned 12 years – his credits too numerous to mention include; film., theatre, television and radio. However, Dinesh cannot keep away for too long and *Fourteen Songs*... is one of many forays back into the Mad Mad world, and hopefully not the last.

Rachel Tanh (Dancer)

Rachel has worked extensively in theatre with her many credits including: *Miss Saigon* (Theatre Royal Drury Lane), *Aladdin* (Brighton Theatre Royal) and *Joseph* (Leicester Haymarket). Her TV and video work includes appearances with Leftfield, Michelle Gayle and guest appearances on various shows and national sports events.

Melody Woodhead (Dancer)

Trained in RAD classical ballet, Melody has an extensive list of dance credits, from pop promotional videos (with acts such as the Spice Girls, Toploader, Lionel Ritchie and Martine McCutcheon) to commercials and road shows.

tamasha

theatre company

Tamasha is one of Britain's leading theatre companies on the national touring circuit. We provide a unique experience of theatre, with stories drawn from the Asian community both in Britain and the Indian sub-continent. Our work traverses beyond the Asian community and is accessible to a growing culturally diverse audience. From adaptations of literature to new commissions, Tamasha has a firm commitment to nurture and produce the work of British Asian writers.

Tamasha was formed in 1989 by Kristine Landon-Smith and Sudha Bhuchar to adapt *Untouchable*, a classic Indian novel by Mulk Raj Anand. Over the past eleven years, the company has produced nine plays, five of which have been adapted for Radio Four and two of which have won the CRE Race in the Media Awards. Their 1997 production, *East is East* transferred to the West End and has since been made into a highly successful film.

Tamasha is funded by the Arts Council of England, London Arts and the London Borough Grants scheme. The company has collaborated with prestigious producing houses including Birmingham Repertory Theatre, the Lyric Theatre Hammersmith, the Royal Court Theatre, the Bristol Old Vic and the Theatre Royal Stratford East.

Artistic Directors	Kristine Landon-Smith & Sudha Bhuchar
General Manager	Bryan Savery
Administrator	Claire Gossop
Fundraising Co-ordinator	Joe Moran
Head of Marketing and PR	Suman Bhuchar
Marketing on behalf of the Lyric	Sam McAuley
Outreach Marketing Co-ordinator	Parminder Dosanjh
Marketing Assistant	Harpreet Kaur
Education Consultant	Sita Brahmachari
Press Consultant	Ben Chamberlain
Marketing Consultant	Mark Slaughter
Production Photographer	Charlie Carter
Bollywood Dance Workshops	Anand Kumar

Tamasha Theatre Company
Unit E, 11 Ronalds Road, London, N5 1XJ
T: 020-7609 2411   F: 020-7609 2722
E: info@tamasha.org.uk   www.tamasha.org.uk
Registered charity number: 1001483

Barclays Stage Partners

Bringing theatre to a wider audience

For more than five years, Barclays Stage Partners has been creating unique, and sometimes unusual opportunities for audiences of all age groups throughout the UK to see top quality theatre.

To date, the scheme has supported 55 productions, touring to over 150 theatres across the UK, reaching an audience in excess of 1 million.

This spring and summer, Barclays Stage Partners, with the Arts Council of England, is supporting tours of *Fourteen Songs, Two Weddings and a Funeral, Honk!* and *The Importance of Being Earnest.*

For details about Barclays Stage Partners call 020 7221 7883

Barclays Bank PLC. Registered Office:
54 Lombard Street, London EC3P 3AH
Registered in England. Registered No. 1026167
Barclays Bank PLC is a member of the
Banking Ombudsman Scheme (UK branches only)

BARCLAYS

THE REP

Birmingham Repertory Theatre

Theatre for the World. Made In Birmingham.

Birmingham Repertory Theatre is one of Britain's leading national theatre companies. From its base in Birmingham, The Rep produces over twenty new productions each year, with shows regularly transferring to London and touring nationally and internationally. In October 1999 The Rep completed a £7.5 million refurbishment which has transformed the theatre, renewed vital stage equipment, increased access and improved public areas.

The commissioning and production of new work lies at the core of The Rep's programme. In 1998 the company launched The Door, a venue dedicated to the production and presentation of new work. This, together with an investment of almost £1 million over four years in commissioning new drama from some of Britain's brightest and best writing talent, gives The Rep a unique position in British theatre. Indeed, through the extensive commissioning of new work The Rep is providing vital opportunities for the young and emerging writing talent that will lead the way in the theatre of the future.

Executive Producer   John Stalker
 Artistic Director   Jonathan Church

Birmingham Repertory Theatre
Centenary Square, Broad Street
Birmingham B1 2EP

Telephone: 0121 245 2000
Fax: 0121 245 2100
www.birmingham-rep.co.uk

Box Office: 0121 236 4455

Registered charity number: 223660

Lyric Theatre Hammersmith

Welcome to the Lyric Theatre Hammersmith.

Hidden away behind a concrete facade on a busy high street, this is one of the most surprising theatres in London. We use it to put on our own shows, and also to make work with a range of award-winning companies from Tamasha to the Royal Shakespeare Company, to host exciting newcomers like Frantic Assembly, The Right Size and Improbable Theatre Company.

When we put on a show, we want to reach as wide an audience as possible. Our education and community programmes, together with our ticket prices, make sure that the doors to the Lyric are open to everyone, in Hammersmith, West London, and beyond.

I hope you enjoy tonight's show, *Fourteen Songs, Two Weddings and a Funeral* and I hope you come back to the Lyric again.

Neil Bartlett, *Artistic Director*

Executive Director
Simon Mellor

Artistic Associates
Tim Albery
Rachel Clare
Michael Morris

Next at the Lyric:

Lyric Theatre Hammersmith & Forkbeard Fantasy presents
Frankenstein - A truly Monstrous Experiment, 7-24 November

Lyric Theatre Hammersmith & Told by An Idiot presents
Aladdin - An Arabian Night Out, 30 November - 12 January

Information & Tickets: 020 8741 2311
email : boxoffice@lyric.co.uk
Web : www.lyric.co.uk

Lyric Theatre Hammersmith is a Registered Charity No. 27851

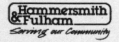

Act One

Overture

Song: 'Is Your Love for Real?'

Prem/Nisha   Is your love for real, or play?
Is your love for real, just say.

I'm never sure when I look at you,
Feel so insecure, could you love me too?
Tell me how do you feel, darling, won't
   you say?
Is your love for real? Is it just for play?
Is your love for real? Is it just for play?

What you mean to me, I'm afraid to tell.
Have some sympathy, it's a magic spell.
In my dreams, you reveal what you never
   say.
Is your love for real? Is it just for play?
Is your love for real? Is it just for play?

Can't we make a start? Can't we know for
   sure?
For my aching heart needs a loving cure.
Only you can heal, end this pain today.
Is your love for real? Is it just for play?
Is your love for real? Is it just for play?

Can't you read my mind? Can't you make
   a guess?
If you could, you'd find love I can't express.
What our hearts conceal, our eyes betray.
Is your love for real? Is it just for play?
Is your love for real? Is it just for play?

Scene One

A cricket pitch – music.
Lalloo *enters and talks to the audience of girls and boys already there.*

Lalloo   Greetings, Namaskar. This is Lalloo Prasad from the Kakaji Stadium. The match is about to begin and I will be providing running commentary throughout. Blue skys – not a cloud to be seen. Pitch inspection is complete and the fielders are in place. Here comes Batsman No. 1 – Karan Shankar. He has played very well this season. He is sure to be 'Man of the Match'. I predict he will be good for a century. And facing him is fast bowler Prem Bhaiya whose spin is faster than Indra, God of wind.

Boy   Hit it for six, Karan!

Girl   Catch him out!

Lalloo   And here he goes – Prem Bhaiya running up to the crease – and it's . . . (*Sound of ball spinning through air.*)

All   . . . OUT!

Boy   You idiot, Karan.

Lalloo   Out for a duck. Very first ball. Karan Shankar out – what a tragedy for the opposition. So – Batsman No. 2 – Gautam Grover is ready to meet fast bowler Prem. Prem moves up to the crease – can he do it again? – here goes . . . Aré vah! Gautam hits it over mid-wicket. Is it a six or will he be caught out? Rita Baby is running to catch it – Run, Rita Baby, run – Oh dear – Oh dear . . .

Music to signal ominous approach of **Bhagwanti**. **Rita** *crashes into* **Bhagwanti**.

Bhagwanti (*falls and screams*)   Oh Bhagwan! Are you trying to kill me?

Arun   Are you all right, Bhagwanti?

Rita   Let me help you. I'm so sorry . . .

Bhagwanti   So you should be.

Lalloo   Oh – hello, Auntie.

Bhagwanti   Don't you dare call me Auntie!

Lalloo   Sorry, Auntie.

Bhagwanti   Huh! God – the way you people treat your servants – they think they own the place.

Karan   Prem – catch you later. We're going to practise over the other side.

Prem   OK – I'll just join you. Lalloo is part of the family, Auntie.

Bhagwanti   What on earth were you all doing anyway?

Prem   Playing cricket, Auntie.

Bhagwanti   Cricket is far too dangerous a sport to be played in the garden. Every Tom, Dick and Harry these days thinks they're Kapil Dev.

Arun   They're kids, Bhagwanti – let them enjoy themselves.

Bhagwanti   Even if I die into the bargain?

Arun (*under breath*)   Chance would be a fine thing.

Bhagwanti   What did you say?

Arun   Nothing, darling.

She exits.

Prem   Uncle, why is Auntie in such a hurry?

Arun   She has been matchmaking. She has a proposal for your brother.

Prem   I don't think Bhaiya's and Auntie's taste is quite the same.

Arun   You know your auntie – she doesn't give up. But don't worry – I also have someone up my sleeve . . .

Prem   Oh – did you hear that, Lalloo? Uncle has found someone for Rajesh.

Lalloo   You mean I'm going to get a bhabi?

Arun   If Prem's Kaka agrees.

Lalloo   I'll go and get the laddoos.

Prem   Who is she, Uncle?

Arun   A very pretty, simple girl.

Prem   But won't Auntie object?

Arun   She's not to know that I have suggested someone.

Prem   But how can you keep it a secret?

Arun   Leave it me, Prem. Now come on – let's go and have some fun.

Scene Two

Interior of **Kaka**'s *house.* **Kaka** *is a rich industrialist and the house reflects his success.* **Kaka** *and* **Bhagwanti** *are walking into the living room.*

Kaka   Bhagwanti – it's so nice to see you. How are you?

Bhagwanti   Fine – apart from being attacked by mad cricketers.

Kaka   Come in – sit down. Where's Arun?

Bhagwanti   Lagging behind as usual.

Kaka   So, to what do we owe this visit? Not that we are not always happy to see you.

Bhagwanti   Well, I was speaking to my brother in Delhi . . .

Kaka   Yes?

Bhagwanti   And I was just saying – you can't praise our Rajesh enough. Managing such a big business at such a young age – it's no joke.

Kaka   Yes – we are all very proud of him.

Bhagwanti   It's high time he got married.

Kaka   And have you got someone in mind?

Bhagwanti   Well, as it happens, my brother's daughter, Sweetie. She's such a pretty girl and so clever.

Arun *and* **Prem** *enter.*

Bhagwanti   Isn't she darling?

Arun   What's that?

Kaka   Bhagwanti was just telling me about her niece, Sweetie.

Arun   Oh yes? The girl is BA failed – too modern – and I hear she's broken off two, maybe three engagements . . .

Bhagwanti   So what? Anyone can make a mistake. Look at me – but it wasn't so easy to break off in our day.

Prem   You'd be lost without Uncle, Auntie.

Bhagwanti   Huh!

Prem   So, is she pretty, this Sweetie?

Bhagwanti   She's rolling in it. You should see their house and the family business is worth carores . . .

Arun   Money isn't everything, darling.

Bhagwanti   You are always interrupting and contradicting me. Here I am, trying to see my nephew settled and you are meddling into something you know nothing about. Just think of the dowry she would bring. Oof! – why am I wasting my time? You are a college professor – your head is in the clouds – what would you know about worldly matters? Bhai Sahib – it would be the most talked about wedding of the season. It would be such a valuable alliance of the two families. Promise me you will think about it before you reject it?

Kaka   Of course I will.

Bhagwanti   Now – I am getting late for my kitty party.

She makes to go. **Lalloo** *enters.*

Lalloo   Auntie – won't you have a laddoo before you go?

Bhagwanti   Not for me.

Lalloo   Oh, I forgot – you are reducing.

Bhagwanti   Donkey! You talk to me like that – what a rude servant. Why don't you sack him at once? Now get out of my way!

She exits. **Prem** *makes to see her out.*

Arun   Kailash Nath – I'm sorry about my wife. As you know, she is totally dazzled by money. Her spoilt niece will not fit in to this family. We want a simple, pretty girl for Rajesh. Someone who will make this house blossom with their love and warmth. And in that one thing I agree with my wife. This house needs a woman. Rajesh and Prem were so young when their parents died – my beloved sister and your respected brother. You left your education halfway through and took on the responsibility of your brother's children. You got a humble job and with hard work as your motto, you are now one of India's leading industrialists.

Kaka   God has been very kind to me.

Arun   You have provided so well for the boys' future. You even sacrificed getting married for their sake. And now it is my turn to do something. I have seen a girl for Rajesh.

Kaka   Aatcha?

Arun   A few days ago, I was in Poona for a conference. There I met a Professor S. S. Chaudhury.

Kaka   Not Siddarth Chaudhury?

Arun   Do you know him?

Kaka   Han – of course. We studied together in college. He was a good friend.

Arun   Aré vah! Well – I met his eldest daughter, Pooja. I saw her only once, but she stayed in my mind. I liked her so much, I asked for her photograph. Here it is.

He hands **Kaka** *the photograph.*

Kaka   Bahut sunder hai . . .

Prem   Let me see, Uncle. Oh – she is pretty!

Arun   Not just pretty. She's BA passed and what a sweet nature.

Kaka   Sounds promising . . .

Arun   I hope so – if they meet and like each other then we can go ahead. At the moment, the Professor is on a pilgrimage at Ram Thakri with his family. As soon as he returns we can go and visit them. He only lives three hours away.

Kaka   But there is one problem, Arun bhai. The moment marriage is mentioned, Rajesh runs a mile.

Prem   Kaka – I have an idea.

Kaka   Yes, beta?

Prem   Why don't we go to Ram Thakri? Rajesh Bhaiya will never suspect our motives for going on a pilgrimage and we'll kill two birds with one stone. God will be satisfied, and you never know, I might get a sister-in-law into the bargain.

Kaka   Good idea.

Arun   Excellent.

Prem   But Rajesh musn't have an inkling. Top secret. Henna Lalloo?

Rajesh *enters.*

Lalloo   Rajesh bhaiya – have a laddoo.

Rajesh   What are we celebrating?

Lalloo   We are all very happy today.

Prem   We've decided on our holiday destination – Ram Thakri.

Rajesh   Ram Thakri?

Prem   Yes.

Rajesh   But Kaka, I thought we were planning on going to a hill station?

Kaka   Yes, but . . .

Lalloo   Ram Thakri is a very sacred place – if you pray there, your dearest wishes will be fulfilled.

Prem   So, programme fixed. Oh, and bhaiya – don't forget to pack your silk kurta.

Rajesh   Why would I need my silk kurta at a holy place?

Prem   You never know . . .

Scene Three

Manager *of hotel at the religious retreat comes on and sets up desk and chair.* **Nisha** *roller-skates on.*

Manager   You always have to enter like a hurricane! Have some respect. The people staying at this guest house have come for a pilgrimage. They want peace.

Nisha   Sorry, Manager Cha Cha.

She takes off her skates.

Manager   Look – can you mind the desk for me for a minute?

Nisha   No problem.

Manager   And do one thing for me – check the total on this bill.

Nisha   Sure.

Manager   And don't get up to any of your tricks

He takes his turban and glasses off and places them on desk. He exits.

Nisha *puts on turban and glasses.*
She starts to add up bill. **Prem** *enters.*

Nisha   Seventy-five plus nine . . .

Prem   Excuse me – is this the Ram Narayan Guest House?

Nisha   Didn't you read the board outside? Oh God – now where was I? Seventy-five plus nine . . .

Prem   Eighty-four.

She gives him a look and then carries on counting. He stands there for a moment and then goes to touch a book lying on the desk. She slaps his hand.

Nisha   So what is it you want?

Prem   Could you please direct me to Professor Chaudhury's room?

Nisha   Why?

Prem   That's for me to know.

Nisha   Oh I see – you people don't study all year round . . .

Prem   I beg your pardon?

Nisha   You don't revise for the whole year and when the exams are round the corner, you chase your professor all the way to a retreat to grovel for more marks.

Prem   I think you need thicker lenses in your glasses, madam. Do I look like a student?

Offstage, **Pooja** *calls out for* **Nisha***.*

Nisha   Oh – Bapré Baap!

She takes off the turban and glasses.

Pooja   Nisha, Nisha!

Nisha   I'm here, didi.

Pooja   What are you doing sitting in the manager's chair?
Mummy's waiting for you.

Nisha   Pooja didi, I was . . .

Manager (*entering with* **Kaka**)   Come in, come in. You
have some luggage?

Kaka   My nephew is getting it out of the car.

Manager   You were asking for Professor Chaudhury?
These are his daughters, Pooja and Nisha. Pooja beti – this
is Mr Kailash Nath – a very old friend of your papa's.

Pooja/Nisha   Namaskar.

Kaka   Namaskar. I see you've already met my second
nephew, Prem.

Pooja   Namaskar.

Prem   Namaskar.

Manager   Pooja – this gentleman wants to meet your
father.

Pooja   I'll take you.

They exit.

Nisha   Here – Manager Cha Cha – I've done the bill.

Prem   I suggest you check that total again. I've heard that
pretty girls often slip up in addition.

Nisha   What did you say?

Prem   Nothing, Nisha ji.

Nisha   Who gave you permission to use my name?

Exit.

Music link.

Scene Four

A room in the ashram's hotel. Sparse, but tasteful.
Professor Chaudhury *enters with food and singing a religious song.* **Kamla**, *his wife, enters a moment later.*

Kamla   Who broke that bowl in the kitchen?

Prof   Taste these lovely kachoris that I made for you. You'll be tempted to break your fast.

Kamla   When will you stop experimenting in the kitchen?

Prof   This is not an experiment, it is a culinary triumph.

Kamla   Who broke that bowl?

Prof   When Lord Ram broke Shiva's bow, his teacher Parshuram, shaking with anger, demanded to know 'Who broke this bow?' and Lord Ram, in a calm and composed manner replied, 'Your humble servant.'

Kamla   Behave yourself. We've got grown-up daughters.

Kaka, **Prem**, **Pooja**, **Nisha** *enter.*

Kaka   Siddarth! – it's been a long time.

Prof   Kailash – is it you? What a pleasant surprise. What a pleasant surprise . . .

Kaka   Kamla – do you recognise me?

Kamla   Of course. Namaste.

Kaka   This is my nephew, Prem.

Prof   Bless you, Prem. This is my wife, Kamla. You know the three of us went to college together? We used to have such fun. You remember Kailash?

Kaka   Of course.

Prof   I see you've met my daughters already . . .

Kaka   Han – lovely girls . . .

Prof   Please come in – sit. We read about you all the time, Kailash – one of India's top industrialists – I'm very proud to be able to say that we were friends in our youth.

Kaka   Oh, come on!

Prof   But Prem – your uncle has certainly lost our bet.

Prem   What's that?

Prof   He used to say that I would lose all my hair before him. And just look at his bald patch!

Kaka   Yes, I have to hand it to you – you have certainly kept your youth.

Prof   So what has brought you here to Ram Thakri? Have you finally turned to God?

Kaka   No, no – a very special mission. If I may be so bold – I would like Pooja for my nephew Rajesh.

Prof   Pooja?

Pooja and **Nisha** *exit.*

Kaka   That is if you don't have any objections . . .

Prof   I couldn't wish for a better home than yours for my daughter.

Kaka   Rajesh is here with us. You must see him first. Prem – go and get your bhaiya.

Prem *leaves.*

Prof   I am indebted to you, Kailash.

Kaka   No, it is me who is indebted to you. I would be honoured if Pooja were to join our family. My business is flourishing, yet our courtyard is empty. So many years without a woman's influence on the boys. As a child, Rajesh at least sat on his mother's lap, but Prem hardly remembers her love.

Prem *and* **Rajesh** *enter.*

Kaka   Ah – here he is. Come on, Rajesh – meet Professor Chaudhury and his wife Kamla.

Rajesh   Namaste.

Musical flourish as we see the girls clocking **Rajesh** *– they approve.*

Kamla (*calling*)   Pooja, Nisha – bring something cold for our guests.

Prof   So, Rajesh – you are in the family business?

Rajesh   Yes, Uncle.

Prof   Have you any other interests?

Prem   Bhaiya is very fond of painting . . .

Prof   Really?

Rajesh   I'm just an amateur . . .

Prem   He's always so modest.

Prof   As it happens, our Pooja is also very fond of painting. Pooja!

Pooja *and* **Nisha** *re-enter with tray of drinks. They hand them round.*

Prof   Pooja – Rajesh is also an artist. Show him the painting you are doing of the temple.

Pooja   Papa – it's nothing special.

Prof   Go on, beti.

She doesn't move.

Prem   Please – he would love to see it – go on, bhaiya . . .

Pooja *and* **Rajesh** *start to go.* **Nisha** *makes to follow.*

Prem   Where are you going?

Nisha   What's that to you?

Prem   Don't be a bone in the kebab. Let them be on their own. You can stay and talk to me.

Nisha   Why would I want to talk to you?

They all now watch **Rajesh** *and* **Pooja***, who have crossed upstairs to look at the painting. In the background, the kachoris are also being passed around.*

Rajesh   This really is a lovely painting.

Pooja   Thank you.

Rajesh   I love the colours you've used.

Pooja   Thank you.

Pause.

Pooja   Have you finished?

Rajesh   Thank you.

Pooja *takes the drink and goes back to the family group to start clearing away the tray of drinks.* **Prem** *approaches* **Rajesh***.*

Prem   Do you like the painting?

Rajesh   Yes, it's good.

Prem   Do you really like the painting?

Rajesh   Yes.

Prem   Do you like the colours in the painting?

Rajesh   Yes.

Prem   Do you like the painter?

Rajesh   Uh . . .

Prem   Come on – what's your verdict?

Rajesh   Uh . . .

Prem   I knew it! I knew it, Kaka – bhaiya's speechless. He's agreed. Now you know why you brought your silk kurta! Congratulations, bhaiya! Everyone – he's agreed – Bhaiya has agreed!

Song: 'Wah Wah Ramji'

Prem   Wah Wah Ramji!
What a couple they'll make.
Bhaiya and Bhabi,
Two swans upon a lake.

Nothing can disguise the light in their eyes,
Blue skies we wish for their sake.

Nisha   We can all share their joy,
The vows they'll never break.
Didi and Jijaji,
A house that stones won't shake.

Nothing can disguise the light in their eyes,
Blue skies we wish for their sake.

Prem   Wah Wah Ramji!

Nisha   Wah Wah Ramji!

Prem   Wah Wah Ramji!

Prem   My brother sitting there,
A cat who got the cream –
Would it be unfair
If I spoilt your dream?

But he's a great guy really,
Yeah, a great guy really.
He's never been in love.
At times a little crazy
But girls, he needs a shove.

Nisha   Take a look at Pooja's smile,
Jokes are just Prem's style.
Didi and Jijaji
So obvious to me.

Both   Nothing can disguise the light in their eyes,
Love's prize – what a ceremony.

Prem   Wah Wah Ramji!

Nisha   Wah Wah Ramji!

Prem   Wah Wah Ramji!

Nisha   Yes, you really have to know
That every day my sister tried
To make her fortune flow,
Bring good luck on to her side.

Oh she prayed so long in temples,
Yes, she prayed so long in temples,
Stayed there every night and day,
Begged the gods to come and help her,
Please to send some love her way.

Prem   The bhabi I'd hoped for me
Sits here just like a dream.

Nisha   Jijaji and Didi,
Two cats who've got the cream.

Both   Nothing can disguise the light in their eyes,
For their sake we wish for blue skies.

Prem   Wah Wah Ramji!

Nisha   Wah Wah Ramji!

Prem   Wah Wah Ramji!

Exit.

Scene Five

Back at **Kaka**'s *house*.

Kaka   Lalloo – is everything prepared for Rajesh's would-be in-laws? They'll be here soon.

Lalloo   Han Kaka. Trust me. It's the first engagement in this house. I won't let you down.

Exits.

Arun   Are you sure Siddarth won't give the game away that I was the go-between?

Kaka   Don't worry.

Arun   You know what Bhagwanti's like – she'll divorce me if she knows I had a hand in it.

Kaka   Everyone is sworn to secrecy.

Arun   Even Lalloo? Are you sure he won't give the game away?

Kaka   Relax – leave it to me.

Bhagwanti *enters*.

Bhagwanti   Congratulations, congratulations! I'm absolutely over the moon about Rajesh's engagement. I was just at the temple. I went to give thanks.

Arun   I thought you were at the beauty parlour, darling.

Bhagwanti   Is it true that the girl's father is a professor?

Kaka   Yes.

Bhagwanti   Well, that rules out any possibility of give and take. Since he's a professor like my husband, he must be a pauper. No question of a dowry.

Arun   Bhagwanti – they are a very respected family.

Bhagwanti   If it was my niece Sweetie, she would have brought so much money. There wouldn't be room in your safe.

Arun   Just be pleased for Rajesh.

Bhagwanti   No, no, I am pleased – I hope they'll be very happy. You rejected all my suggestions – you wanted a simple girl. What can I do? Where did you find her?

Prem   Ah – a friend of a friend of a friend found her for us.

Bhagwanti   Friends' suggestions are taken before family's!

Kaka   Rajesh himself approved the girl.

Bhagwanti   He might have approved Sweetie if you'd allowed them to meet! So, who is this friend of a friend of a friend? He organised things pretty quickly.

Prem   No one that you know, Auntie.

Bhagwanti   Arun – do you know the fellow?

Arun   No – no. I am a simple professor – my nose is always buried in a book. Who do I meet?

Lalloo *enters.*

Lalloo   They're here – the car's just pulled up.

Arun   Bhagwanti, don't say anything out of turn.

Bhagwanti   As if I would.

Kaka   Come on – let's go and greet them.

Nisha *runs on.*

Nisha   Hello – Namaste, Uncle.

Kaka   Welcome, beti. Let me introduce you. This is Nisha, Pooja's younger sister, this is Rajesh's Mama, Arun and his wife, Bhagwanti. And this is our Lalloo – he is part of the family.

Nisha   Namaste. Namaste. Where's my would-be brother-in-law? Pooja didi has sent something for him. I can't wait to give it to him.

Prem   He's upstairs getting ready.

Kaka   Prem – look after Nisha. We must go and greet her parents.

Others exit.

Nisha   Wow – you didn't tell me you had such a beautiful house!

Prem   Did my bhabi send me anything?

Nisha   Well, I tried my utmost to discourage her, but she insisted.

Nisha *takes out a packet.* **Prem** *unwraps it.*

Prem   Wow – a brooch!

Nisha   Put it on your jacket. It'll impress your girlfriends.

Prem   Nisha ji – could I ask you to put it on for me?

She does so.

Prem   Ouch!

Nisha   Sorry – did I prick you?

Prem   No.

Nisha   Then why did you scream?

Prem   Just wanted to see . . .

Nisha   What?

Prem   Nothing.

Nisha   Nearly done. (*She pricks him.*)

Prem   Ouch – that really did hurt.

Nisha   Sorry.

Prem   You did it on purpose . . .

Nisha   Me?

Prem   Why?

Nisha   Just wanted to see . . .

Prem   What?

Nisha   Nothing.

Prem   You know, after today's ceremony we'll be related. Who will you be to me?

Nisha   I'll be your sister-in-law's sister and you'll be my brother-in-law's brother.

Prem   Not just pretty, but smart. Very smart.

Rajesh *and* **Two Boys** *enter.*

Boy   Hi, Prem! Are we late?

Nisha   Jijaji – hi!

Rajesh   Nisha – how are you?

Nisha   I'm so happy to be here. Didi sent this gift for you.

Prem   Don't open it yet – it might bite!

Kaka, **Kamla**, **Professor**, **Lalloo**, **Arun**, **Bhagwanti** *and* **Two Girls** *enter.* **Lalloo** *brings the luggage and* **Kamla** *and* **Arun** *carry a tray and lots of presents. They all greet each other.*

Prof   Come on, Kamla. We are here for the engagement – let's do what we came for. Put the tilak on the boy's forehead. I'm impatient to welcome him into our family.

Music to underscore ceremony.
Tilak on forehead. **Rajesh** *touches* **Kamla**'*s feet.*

Kamla   Jitay raho beta.

She gives him gifts and a laddoo.

Prof   Now Rajesh is ours. Come here, yaar. (*To* **Kaka**.)
Let's embrace – this is the last time we'll hug as equals.

Kaka   What do you mean?

Prof   We are from the girl's side. From now on we'll be
forever bowing to you.

Kaka   Don't be silly. (*They embrace.*)

Arun   Don't think you can get away with just an embrace.
Now that you're all related, we want some entertainment!
Let's have some singing.

All   Good idea.

Bhagwanti   Who is going to start?

Kaka   How about you, Siddarth?

Prof   Me? You're the one with the voice.

Kaka   That was a long time ago . . .

Prem   You used to sing, Kaka? You kept that quiet.

Prof   In those days he had good reason to sing. Don't be
embarrassed, Kamla. Look at that smile – it's bewitching
even today, but in those days, people went crazy just to get a
glimpse of it. And amongst those whose heartbeat
quickened at her smile, was none other than your Kaka!

Kaka   No. No – it wasn't like that . . .

Prof   Come on now – don't try to deny it. Come on, yaar.
Sing something about that smile like you used to.

All   Yes. Yes – come on, Kaka!

Kaka   You're all mad! Rajesh – put some sense into your
father-in-law's head.

Rajesh   I'm staying out of this.

All   Come on – sing, Uncle!

Prof   Kamla – why don't you try and twist his arm? He won't say no to you.

Kamla   Please sing something.

Song: 'Beauty Stands Before Me'

Kaka   Beauty stands before me,
Still can overawe me,
And here she stands asking me to sing.
How can I refuse her?
Beauty can choose anything.

Eyes as bright as diamonds,
Her hair flows down like a river stream,
Drowning in her beauty,
Waving me on through a dream.

Skin is softer than silk,
Smile as bright as midday sun.
Skin is softer than silk,
Smile as bright as midday sun.

I was one voice of many,
Singing to Kamla's beauty.
Like a pair of young lovers,
With each look he discovers,
That he's a very lucky man.
Even today she makes his heart skip,
And spin around
As fast as it can.

All   With each look he discovers,
That he's a very lucky man.
Even today she makes his heart skip,
And spin around
As fast as it can.

Prem   Come on, Auntie – let's have an answer!

Kamla   Here he stands before me,
Here he stands before me,
And from the past, bells are ringing.
Then he'd just adore me,
Now we both sit here singing.

Delicately tying,
The long threads of two families.
There is no denying,
Love is more than just fantasies.

She is the sun in my sky,
See my look in her eye.
She is the sun in my sky,
See my look in her eye.
She's my pleasure and joy,
Now she'll treasure this boy.

When they look at each other,
When they look at each other,
She wears her youth like pure gold.
When they're with one another,
May their love never grow cold.

All   When they look at each other,
She wears her youth like pure gold.
When they're with one another,
May their love never grow cold.

Everyone applauds and **Lalloo** *brings on more laddoos.*

Nisha   Lalloo – come over here with that tray.

She goes to **Rajesh** *with a laddoo.*

Nisha   Rajesh?

Rajesh   Yes, Nisha ji?

Nisha   Open your mouth.

Rajesh   What?

Nisha   Here – try this delicious laddoo.

She stuffs his mouth with it.

Nisha   Wasn't it good?

Prem   Don't overdo it now. What will you offer us when we come to your house for the wedding?

Nisha   Oh, don't worry – you'll see our hospitality . . .

Prem   So, when we arrive – there'll be fireworks!

Music, which cross-fades to sound of fireworks, takes us to next scene. The music here is that of a brass band playing in the groom's procession of the wedding.

Scene Six: At the Professor's house for the wedding

The **Girls** *are on a balcony overlooking the procession.*
Noise of excited crowd outside.

Nandini   I can't see the groom. The procession's in the way.

Rita   There he is – on the white horse.

Nandini   His face is hidden by all the flowers. Is he handsome, Nisha?

Nisha   I can assure you my brother-in-law is quite a catch.

Radha   Who is that young guy prancing around in front of everyone?

Nisha   That's Prem – Rajesh's younger brother.

Radha   He's cute.

Nisha   Don't tell him that – he already thinks he's God's gift to women. Right – girls – ready to show them how hospitable we can be?

All   Yes!

Nisha   This is the strategy: the minute Rajesh takes off his shoes for the ceremony, one of us grabs them when no one's watching.

Nandini   That'll be easy.

Brass band comes to an end.

Nisha   Don't underestimate that Prem – the boys from the Baraat will be on their guard.

Radha   How much money should we ask from Rajesh for his shoes?

Nisha   We'll start at five thousand and go from there . . .

Girls *exit.*
Cross-fade, so the sound becomes interior chat and a small band.

Prem, **Lalloo** *and* **Four Boys** *run on.* **Prem** *is carrying a mithai box.*

Prem   So, Karan – give me Rajesh's shoes.

He places them in box.

Dilip   A1 idea of yours, Prem.

Prem   Han – the last place the girls will think of looking is in this mithai box. We must guard it with our lives. Theek hai?

All   Theek hai.

As they are leaving, **Rita** *approaches.*

Rita   Oh, Prem! You didn't need to bring your own mithai – we have plenty to go around.

Prem   It's a special mithai for my aunt – she's diabetic.

Rita   Oh, I see. Shall I take it for you and put it in the fridge?

Prem   No, thank you – I'll hang on to it . . . in case she suddenly wants some.

Rita   OK.

Boys *leave*. **Nisha** *enters*.

Nisha   Anything to report?

Rita   Bull's eye! The shoes are in the red mithai box that Prem is guarding with his life.

Nisha   Touché. Now we need to make a plan . . . how to get them! Come on.

Lalloo *and* **Prem** *come on with box.*
They sit. We imagine they are now in the centre of the wedding.
Lalloo *is drumming on the box.*

Lalloo   Prem Bhaiya. You're very clever. No one would ever guess that the shoes are in this box.

Prem   Keep quiet, Lalloo – we are in enemy territory now.

Lalloo   But we have won. The bride is now arriving . . .

Prem   The show isn't over yet. I don't trust my brother's sali and her green duppatta gang.

Nandini *enters*.

Nandini   Are you Prem?

Prem   Yes.

Nandini   There's a phone call for you.

Prem   For me? Who is it?

Nandini   A lady. She said she wanted to speak to Prem.

Prem   OK – I'm just coming.

Prem *leaves with* **Nandini**. **Radha** *enters*.

Radha   Excuse me.

Lalloo   Yes?

Radha   The gentleman who was sitting with you. He wants you.

Lalloo   He wants me where?

Radha   He's on the phone. He said to come straight away.

Lalloo   Oh, OK then – I'm coming.

He exits with **Radha** *and absent-mindedly leaves the box.* **Nisha** *and* **Nandini** *come on and swap boxes.*

Nandini   Quick – swap them now! No one's watching . . .

Nisha   I never knew Rita was such a good actress. She's kept Prem on the phone for quite a while.

Nandini   He really believes she's an ex-girlfriend!

Nisha   I told you, he thinks of himself as a Casanova. Come on – now let's go and hide it.

Prem *walks on with a cordless phone.*

Prem   Look, how many times do I have to tell you – I don't recall meeting you, but I'm sorry if I broke your heart. Oooh – she was chattering away – now she's hung up! I'll never understand women.

Lalloo *enters.*

Prem   Lalloo – what are you doing here?

Lalloo   You called me.

Prem   No. Where's the box?

They run off and back to the box.

Lalloo   Ooof – that was a close shave.

Prem   I told you to keep alert. Don't let me down again.

Lalloo *opens box.*

Lalloo   Prem bhaiya – I don't know how to say this, but the shoes have turned into sweets . . .

Prem   What?

Lalloo   See for yourself.

Prem (*reading a note from inside the box*)   'One expects to find mithai in a mithai box. Hope it's sweet enough for you.' Lalloo – we've been had! Come on.

They exit. **The Girls** *run up to the balcony.*

Nisha   Let's hide them here. Everyone's seated for the ceremony – no one's going to come up here.

Karan *walks past underneath the balcony, whistling.*

Nandini   Ssh! There's someone down below . . .

Karan   Hi, Nisha. I have something to show you for Pooja.

Nisha   I'm sure she'll like whatever it is.

Karan   No – come down. I want your opinion.

Nisha *comes down.* **Karan** *asks her to hold his box while he unwraps the gifts – then an elaborate swapping of boxes which confuses* **Nisha** *and leaves* **Karan** *with the shoe box.* **Karan** *exits in triumph, then the* **Girls** *exit.*
Lalloo, **Prem** *and* **Boys** *enter.*

Prem   These girls have made fools of us.

Lalloo   Don't give up so easily. (*He prays to the Lord Krishna locket which he wears around his neck*): Lord – you are a master of miracles. We are in desperate need of one now – we have lost the last round – please let us regain our ground, so that we are the winners and they end up looking like owls.

Gautam   You think you'll rub your little charm and Krishna will appear to get Rajesh's shoes back?

Lalloo   Have faith.

Karan (*from offstage*)   'Lalloo, my loyal devotee, you prayed for me and I am here – look up and see your miracle.'

He enters and dangles the shoes.

All Vah – bhai. Thank you, Lord Krishna. Good work.

Prem Great work. Come on – come down – the ceremony is about to begin.

They exit. Lighting change. Religous wedding chant in background. **Pooja** *and* **Rajesh** *in wedding dress walk on and round an imaginary fire. Rose petals fall from the ceiling. This is a stylised moment. They slowly walk off.*

Girls *and* **Boys** *enter: boys led by* **Karan**, *girls by* **Nisha**.

Girls Never. Never – not on your life!

Karan Fifteen hundred rupees – that's all we're offering.

Nisha Fifteen hundred! We've asked for five thousand.

Karan Two thousand and not a rupee more.

Girls Not on your life!

Nisha My sister is going into a stingy household.

Karan Take it or leave it.

Nisha OK – let Rajesh sit there with bare feet. He's not getting his shoes for that price.

Karan It's our final offer.

Nisha Prem – doesn't your brother want his shoes? Why don't you negotiate?

Prem No. No – you strike a deal with Karan – he is our spokesperson.

Nisha OK, OK – we can see you're tight. We're not unreasonable. Three thousand. What do you say, girls?

Girls Theek Hai.

Karan Two thousand five hundred.

Nisha Cash!

Dilip God, these girls are fast!

Nisha/Girls   Cash!

Prem   It's time I intervened. My brother will give you cash, but we want to see what we're paying for first.

Nisha   You'll get the shoes. Don't you trust us?

Prem   Well, bring them. You give me the shoes – we'll give you the money – straight swap.

Nisha   OK – follow me, girls.

They cross to balcony.
From below:

Prem   Don't look – let's see what she does.

Karan   She'll have to admit defeat.

Prem   If I know Nisha, she'll never do that.

Karan   So what do we do?

Prem   Leave it to me. Where did you hide the shoes, Karan?

Karan   Just behind the curtains . . .

Nisha   Shit! (*She's seen shoes are not there.*)

Radha   What's happened?

Nisha   We've been had!

Radha   What do we do?

Nisha   Look casual.

Prem   Got the shoes, Nisha ji? (*Counting money.*) I've got the cash.

Nisha   Han – they're in this box.

Prem   Let me see.

Nisha   Mmm mmm – money first.

Prem   Mmmm mmm – you give us the shoes – then you take the money.

Song: 'Shoes for Cash'

Boys   Hey Hey!
Hey Hey!
Hey Hey!

Prem   You stand there mocking us, now sisters you may feel
Your tricks are shocking us, but now we have to do
a deal.
So give the shoes, girls,
You can't refuse, girls.

Boys   Then take our cash, girls.
It's quite a stash, girls

Girls   Hey Hey!
Hey Hey!

Nisha   You boys look so hard done by – you shouldn't be
too sad.
The shoes have both been won by us – you should
be feeling glad.
They'll be returning,
Once we are earning.

Girls   Just pay the cash, boys,
You've got a stash, boys.

Boys   First give the shoes, girls,
You can't refuse, girls.

Boys   Hey Hey!

Girls   Hey Hey!

Nisha   Count your money.
Prem   We refuse.
Nisha   Every penny.
Prem   First the shoes.
Nisha   We won't cheat you.
Prem   We can't wait.
Nisha   We will beat you.
Prem   Trust in fate.

Boys   Let's be blunt,
            It's the shoes up front.
Nisha   We'll raise the price.
Prem   Getting vicious.
Nisha   No, we're nice.
Prem   We're suspicious.
Nisha   Our word's enough.
Prem   But we agreed.
Nisha   I'd say that's tough.
Prem   It's shoes we need.

Boys   It's shoes we need.

Nisha   No need to shout and roar – the shoes are just our
            little joke.
            Will you call in the law, or are you all completely
            broke?
            Not being funny, we want your money.

Girls   Don't try to sweeten,
            We've got you beaten.

Boys   Just get the shoes, boys,
            They can't refuse, boys.
            Hey Hey!
            Hey Hey!
            Hey Hey!
            Hey Hey!
            Hey Hey!
            Hey Hey!
            Just give the shoes, girls,
            You can't refuse, girls.

            Repeat.

Radha *finds the shoes, shouts 'Nisha' and throws them to her. A battle over the shoes ensues between* **Prem** *and* **Nisha** *who grabs them and runs upstairs.* **Prem** *follows. He grabs* **Nisha** *and suddenly the battle changes to love.* **Prem** *and* **Nisha** *stare at each other.* **Prem** *allows* **Nisha** *to keep the shoes and the dance resumes as* **Nisha** *comes down to claim her money before handing over the shoes.*

Scene Seven

All are assembled downstairs to say goodbye to **Pooja**. **Nisha** *puts the shoes on* **Rajesh***'s feet.*

Song: 'My Ship is Leaving'

Pooja   Whatever you've taught me, my father,
Today now has brought me
A life among a new family.

I'm leaving today for a new life,
I'm going away as a wife,
And as I go, I want you to know
I love you.
There'll be no one above you,
Not even in my new family.

Happy, yet I'm sad at departing,
But I'm starting a new day.
Mother, be joyful, no grieving.
My ship is leaving,
Sailing away.
Sister, don't cry, be strong now,
It won't be long now
Before you're with a new family.

They all exit. On the way out, **Prem** *stops* **Nisha**.

Prem   Nisha ji – I just wanted to apologise.

Nisha   What for?

Prem   I'm sorry if I went too far today.

Nisha   Not at all.

Prem   With all the laughter and leg-pulling – I hope you'll forgive me if I offended you in any way . . .

Nisha   There's nothing to forgive.

Prem   I assure you it was all meant in fun.

Nisha   I know.

Prem   I'll make sure Pooja bhabi is surrounded by so much love that she won't be able to dwell on the sadness of leaving her home.

Nisha   Thank you, Prem.

They exit.

Scene Eight

Time has passed. **Pooja** *enters first – she is nine months pregnant. Others follow and set up the scene for tea.* **Bhagwanti**, **Arun**, **Kaka**, **Nisha**, **Prem**, **Rajesh**, **Lalloo** *are present.*

Arun   Bhagwanti – you look like 'Pretty Woman' with that hairdo. My wife is getting younger and I am getting older.

Bhagwanti   Do you really think so, Arun?

Lalloo   Han, Auntie ji – Uncle is right. When you were sitting just now, from behind even I mistook you for Nisha ji!

Bhagwanti   Thank you, Lalloo.

Lalloo   But the minute you got up – of course I knew it was you.

Bhagwanti   Cheeky rascal! Kailash Nath – see how your servant speaks to me?

Kaka   Lalloo – give Auntie a cup of tea.

Lalloo   Auntie ji – I have brought for you something very fresh and refreshing to drink.

Kaka   Aré vah! Pooja – since you have been teaching Lalloo, he's become a real gentleman.

Bhagwanti   Gentleman! Huh! What would a monkey know about the taste of ginger?

Lalloo   Oh yes, Auntie ji – this is for you. It is ginger tea.

Arun   See how smart he is?

Bhagwanti   So, Pooja beti – how are you feeling? Delivery could be any time now, henna?

Pooja   I'm fine, Auntie.

Arun   So, Kailash – you're a would-be grandfather?

Kaka   As it is, Siddarth teases me in his letters that since Pooja has come into this house, I have taken to wearing a dhoti and listening to her recite the Ramayana. After the baby is born, his jokes will be relentless.

Nisha   Well, you can tease him back, you know. He too will be an old grandfather!

They all laugh.

Prem   I feel bad. Because of me, bhaiya is having to go abroad on business at such an important time . . .

Rajesh   Pagla . . .

Prem   Her delivery could be at any time – she needs you on this occasion.

Rajesh   Look what your brother-in-law is saying, Pooja.

Pooja   What's he saying?

Rajesh   He's saying that you could deliver at any time and that it's his fault that I'm having to go abroad.

Pooja   Is there a better friend to a bhabi, than her brother-in-law?

Pooja *and* **Prem** *hug.*

Pooja   Prem – your Kaka, your bhaiya and I, we all share a dream that one day you'll be successful in business. Once your brother meets the foreign collaborators, your factory can be established and then you can make a name for yourself. You will be here. Why do I have to worry that Rajesh is not?

Kaka   Pooja is truly one in a million. She has brought so much wealth to this house.

Bhagwanti   My Sweetie would have brought a lot more . . .

Arun   There are many daughter-in-laws, Bhagwanti, who would resent the boy's attachment to his family.

Nisha   See, Rajesh – what a catch you've got!

Rajesh   With a sali like you – what can I do but agree?

Nisha   And what do you mean by that, 'a sali like me'?

Rajesh   Your hard bargaining for my shoes at the wedding has taught me never to cross you. Prem – learn from this – don't marry someone who's got a firecracker for a sister. Marry an only girl.

Prem   I will marry whoever my bhabi chooses for me. Henna bhabi?

Pooja   Of course. Without my approval, you can't get married. And you touch my feet every day and then I'll see what I can do.

Prem   Anything you say, bhabi.

Pooja   I am the elder daughter-in-law. I'll find someone that I can boss around.

Prem   My fate is in your hands, but I do have one request.

Pooja   What's that, Prem?

Prem   That she should be everything that you are.

Arun   See how devoted he is to his bhabi?

Nisha   Han – any request of hers, he fulfils.

Pooja   Nisha!

Prem   What's that supposed to mean?

Nisha   She craved for something spicy – instead, you brought her sweet laddoos.

Prem   But she enjoyed them . . .

Nisha   But it's not what she asked for!

Prem   Pooja bhabi – didn't you enjoy them?

Pooja   I'm staying out of this.

Nisha   When she asked for lemon, you brought her melon!

Prem   We want this baby to be sweet-natured, not sour like you!

Nisha   Ahhhh! See how he talks about our family?

Prem   Only joking . . .

Nisha   Watch it!

Song: 'Didi, This New Brother-in-Law is Crazy!'

Nisha   La la la la la la la
La la la la la la la

Didi, this new brother-in-law is crazy.
Never been another who's more crazy.
Plays the clown, trying to impress us.

All   Brings us down, it's starting to depress us!

Nisha   He always plays a joke, playing tricks for kisses.
He's aiming to provoke, but he always misses.
Brings us down, it's starting to depress us,

All   Plays the clown, just trying to impress us!

Nisha   La la la la la la la la la la

All   La la la la la la la la la la

Nisha   She asks for a favour,
             He says it's a pleasure.
             The wrong things he brings her,
             Then says that it's treasure.
             She just couldn't trust him
             To turn up when told to.
             Don't try to rely on,
             His word he can't hold to.
             Someone please tell the boy he's maddening.
             He really isn't well – it's all so saddening.
             Plays the clown, trying to impress us.

All   Brings us down, it's starting to depress us.

Nisha   Hai hai hai hai
             Didi, I'm sure Prem's really crazy,
             Brings us down, it's starting to depress us.

All   La la la la la la la la la la la

Nisha   La la la la la la

Prem   Bhabi dear, I'm dazzled by your sister.
             She leaves us all too frazzled to resist her.
             No more clown, if my jokes just distress her,
             Wear a frown whenever I address her.

             Someone help me please, come now and save
             me, I'm quaking at the knees from the look she
                gave me.
             It's no use if my jokes just distress her,
             I've no excuse, I don't want to depress her.

             Pa pa pa pa pa pa pa pa
             If the list that she gave me
             Was wrong, then I'll pay you.
             Be my judge, but save me,
             Show mercy, what say you?

             So punish me, will you?
             Whatever you say –
             I'll follow,
             until you send me away.

Will that put an end to your objections?
I'll just bend to all of your directions
I'll obey – stop trying to impress you

Women   From today?

Prem   Stop trying to depress you.

Rajesh   Ooh – I'm scared. I hope we have a boy.

Pooja   Ooh no – I'm already out-numbered in this house!

Kaka   Aah, Nisha. Since you've come here to look after your sister, there is such an atmosphere of fun in this house. We won't let you go home that easily. Henna Prem?

Prem   Nisha ji might have commitments to get back to.

Nisha   What commitment is greater than being with my sister at this time?

Prem   So you'll stay?

Nisha   For as long as she needs me.

Arun   OK, Rajesh. Are you ready? We'll get you to the airport. The sooner you go, the sooner you are back.

Kaka   I am also coming to see you off.

Rajesh   Kaka, there is no need.

Kaka   No, no – I insist.

Arun   Come on, Bhagwanti – otherwise Rajesh will miss his plane.

Bhagwanti   Don't forget my shopping list, Rajesh.

Arun   I'm sure Rajesh has better things to do than pick up your lipsticks!

Bhagwanti   He is my nephew. Of course he'll be happy to do it. Please don't come back without Revlon's 'Russet Gold'.

Rajesh   Han Auntie – don't worry, I'll get what you want. Prem, look after Pooja for me.

Prem   Of course, bhaiya.

Prem *and* **Rajesh** *hug.*

Pooja   Don't forget to phone every day.

Rajesh   I won't.

General goodbyes and they leave.

Pooja   I think I'll go and lie down.

Lalloo   Shall I bring you anything, bhabi?

Pooja   Nahin – thank you. Nisha – if Prem needs anything, will you see to it?

Nisha   Yes, didi.

She exits. **Lalloo** *starts to tidy up.*

Lalloo   Prem bhaiya – have you tried this halwa? It's A1. Nisha ji made it.

Prem   Really? I didn't realise you could cook.

Nisha   Try some.

He takes it.

Prem   It's delicious. This is my favourite dish. How did you know?

She winks at **Lalloo**.

Prem   So, Lalloo had a hand in it?

Lalloo   She asked a simple question 'What is Prem's favourite food?' I just gave the answer.

Lalloo *exits.*

Prem   I am already a fan of your singing and dancing. Now I'm a fan of your cooking.

Nisha   You didn't mind me teasing you just now?

Prem   Why would I mind?

Nisha Well – I painted you as quite an idiot, but it was all meant in fun.

Prem And it was taken in fun.

Nisha Good.

Prem I also joined in. You know, you are the only person I can take such liberties with?

Nisha Really?

Prem Yes. I don't mind anything that you say or do . . .

Nisha Why? Why with me? Who am I to you?

He takes another bite of halwa.

Prem This is the most tasty halwa I've ever had.

Nisha I'm glad you like it.

Prem Why did you make my favourite food? Who am I to you?

Nisha You shouldn't talk with your mouth full.

Prem You haven't answered my question.

Nisha You didn't answer mine . . .

Song: 'Just a Mere Glance'

Prem Just a mere glance from me to you,
Could be sheer chance, it could be true.
This romance, is something new.
Love is a trance, what can I do?
So familiar, yet so unknown,
Can I make this love my own?
Just a glance and it's so true,
Love is a dance and made for two.
One look to me,
See, surprise in shimmering eyes, gazing at me.
Now I'm all at sea,
Swept by a wave,

A gaze of secret, deepest passions set me free.
And now I'm her slave.
It's clearer than words on a page
The nearer I get to this stage.
Oh oh oh
Just a mere glance and it's so true,
Love is a dance and made for two.

Oh my Nisha,
She's the star that guides me to a magic land.
My bright Nisha,
She will be there to take
All the threads of my life in her gentle hand
And they won't break.
Some lives are changed by a book,
Mine's rearranged with a look.
Oh oh oh
Just a mere glance from me to you,
Could be sheer chance, it could be true.
This romance is something new,
Love is a dance and made for two.

They are just about to kiss.

Lalloo (*off*)   Prem bhaiya! Prem bhaiya!

Prem   What is it, Lalloo?

Lalloo   Call the doctor – the baby's coming!

Blackout.

Act Two

Scene One

Music. Car trucks on and **Prem**, **Rajesh**, **Pooja** *and* **Baby** *are by the car loading it up.* **Bhagwanti** *is also there.*

Bhagwanti   Make sure you come back soon. We don't want Munna to forget his home.

Pooja   Yes, Auntie. Why don't you come with us, Rajesh? Nisha always writes that Mummy and Daddy are missing you.

Rajesh   Tell them that when I come to fetch you, I'll stay for a while. And tell your sister to behave herself in front of Munna. I don't want any bad influences on my boy.

Pooja   Take care of yourself. Eat properly.

Rajesh   Don't worry about me.

Pooja   But I do.

Prem   Aatcha Aatcha – lovebirds. It's only a short separation. You don't have to linger over the goodbyes.

Lalloo (*entering*)   Pooja bhabi – this telegram has just come for me. It's from my village. Will you read it to me?

She opens it.

Prem   What is it, bhabi?

Pooja   Your mother isn't well, Lalloo – she's in hospital. You should go at once.

Lalloo   What has happened?

Pooja   It doesn't say, but hopefully it's nothing too serious. Go on today's bus and take this money with you.

Bhagwanti   Why are you giving him money?

Pooja   So he can get his mother treated.

Bhagwanti   These servants. This illness is just an excuse to get money out of you.

Pooja   What are you saying, Auntie?

Bhagwanti   You can buy a telegram like this for five bucks. You give him that money and that'll be the last you see of him.

Lalloo   I swear to you, bhabi – this telegram is not fake. I didn't buy it. I'm being wrongly accused because I'm a small man!

Pooja   Since when have you become small? Now, Lalloo – you think of me as your bhabi henna?

Lalloo   Yes, bhabi.

Pooja   Keep this money and go on today's bus.

Bhagwanti   When will you people learn about the role of servants? He's taking you for a ride.

Bhagwanti *exits.*

Lalloo   Bhabi – I'm scared. If anything happens to my mother what will I do?

Pooja   Have faith. I know nothing will go wrong. I'll pray for her.

Rajesh   Come on – I'll take you to the bus station, Lalloo.

Lalloo   No, no – you'll be late for the office. I'll be fine.

Pooja   Come on, Lalloo – go quickly now. Your mother will be needing you.

Lalloo   Thank you, Pooja bhabi. I feel better now that you will be praying for her.

Pooja *gets into the car –* **Lalloo** *goes round to* **Prem**'s *side.*

Pooja   Rajesh, see that Lalloo gets to the bus station quickly.

Rajesh   Don't worry – I'll take him

Lalloo   Prem bhaiya – See how understanding our bhabi is? You tell her your heart's secret – she'll be happy for you.

Prem   Take care of yourself, Lalloo. All set?

The car starts up. Goodbyes and waves. **Rajesh** *and* **Lalloo** *go inside.*

Music: 'Mausam Ka Jadu' plus SFX of car.

After a while:

Pooja   So why are you so happy today? I'm the one who's going home after such a long time.

Prem   Bhabi – I love you.

Pooja   Prem – stop fooling around. I want to have a serious chat with you. Kaka ji has given me the responsibility of settling you now that your factory is established. What do you think?

Prem   Sure – of course . . .

Pooja   So, do you want an arranged marriage or a love match?

Prem   It will be a love match that you will arrange for me.

Pooja   What is all this?

Prem   I love you, bhabi.

Pooja   You see, Munna? Quietly, quietly – your Uncle Prem has found a chachi for you.

Prem   Oh – Munna approves of his chachi-to-be. Isn't that right?

Pooja   What?

Prem   Munna has seen the photograph. Tell your mother what you think.

Baby *chuckles.*

Prem   You see? He agrees with me.

Pooja   Why haven't you shown me the photo?

Prem   Because you're going to meet her in person.

Pooja   Oh – does she live on the way?

Prem   Yes, bhabi – don't worry – she's on the way.

Music continues to show passing of time. Car finally stops. Music fades.

Pooja   Well, we're home. I have reached my destination. But where is your heart's destination?

Prem   Bhabi – you and my heart have the same destination.

Pooja   Nisha!

They get out of car – car trucks off. They go inside.

Prem   Bhabi – welcome. Think of this as your own home!

They sit – there is a note lying on the coffee table.

Pooja   So – tell me everything . . .

Prem   Read this note first.

*She opens it but before she can read it, **Prem** recites if off by heart.*

Prem   'Mama and Papa have gone out – they won't be back till evening. Relax – have something to eat. Nisha.'

Pooja   I get it – you and your madam have hatched this plan. Ah, what love is!

Nisha *is hiding, listening to all this.*

Pooja   Chal, chal – call your brother in his office straight away! Let's break the happy news.

Prem   Let me bow down and touch your feet, Bhabi.

Pooja   Just go and dial Rajesh.

Prem *goes downstairs and dials **Rajesh**.*

Prem *(on phone)*   Hello, is bhaiya there? He's out?

Pooja   Leave a message . . .

Prem   Tell him to phone his wife as soon as he gets in.
She's at her mother's home. Thank you.

Pooja *takes off her necklace.* **Prem** *goes back upstairs.*

Pooja   I want you to give your mother's necklace to Nisha
in front of me.

Prem   How can I, bhabi? Your sister is so shy – she's not
coming out.

Pooja   OK. If she won't come out, we'll have to persuade
her. We'll form a procession and take her. After all, we are
from the boy's side. We're not budging without a promise
from the bride!

Song: 'Here I Go'

Nisha *eventually comes out and joins in and* **Prem** *puts the
necklace on her at the end of the song.*

Pooja   Here I go,
　　　　　Here I go,
　　　　　With my Devarji's wedding procession.
　　　　　Here I go,
　　　　　Here I go,
　　　　　Leading the wedding procession.
　　　　　Here I go,
　　　　　No band, no music, only good wishes
　　　　　Straight from my heart I bring.
　　　　　Here I go,
　　　　　Heading the wedding procession.
　　　　　Here I go,
　　　　　Devar will be addressing
　　　　　A bridegroom so impressing.
　　　　　Me, bhabi, will be in front to show the way.
　　　　　May all their days be shining,
　　　　　Jewels on a necklace entwining.
　　　　　Precious wishes I bring to you on your marriage day.
　　　　　Groom proudly riding,

So bride is hiding.
We've come to take you away.
Here I go.

Wah wah Ramji!
What a couple they'll make,
Joy to all the family.
The chain of love will never break,
Nothing can disguise the light in their eyes,
Blue skies I wish for their sake.

Now this day will make me
The eldest of us, but don't take me
As I was before, young sister-in-law.
You must obey.
With my words I command you,
With stares and glares I demand you.
Watch what you do,
I'm set above you on your marriage day.

What can I give to show?
I want you to know
My happiness, so don't delay.
Here I go,
Here I go with my Devarji's wedding procession,
Here I go.

The phone rings.

Pooja   That must be Rajesh!

Pooja *runs off to get phone. As she runs downstairs, she trips and falls dramatically down the stairs, underscored by music.*

Prem/Nisha   Didi! Bhabi!

Scene Two

A hospital bed trucks on. **Pooja** *is in bed.* **Prem**, **Nisha**, **Kamla**, **Professor**, **Kaka** *and a* **Doctor** *are all around the bed.* **Rajesh** *enters.*

Pooja *opens her eyes. She looks at* **Prem** *and* **Nisha**. **Prem** *and* **Nisha** *look at each other.* **Pooja** *points at* **Prem** *and* **Nisha**.

Prof   Doctor – my daughter is trying to say something . . .

A bleep increases. Dramatic tension heightens. A feeling of panic sets in.

Prof   What's the matter, Dr Sahib?

Doctor   Her heart rate is decreasing.

Kamla   Please, Doctor – help my daughter!

Machine bleeps and then the signal fades.

Kaka   Doctor, what's happened?

Doctor   I'm sorry . . .

Screams and cries – music as the hospital bed is wheeled off.

Scene Three

Sound of rickshaw pulling up. **Lalloo** *comes on with bags and luggage.*

Lalloo   Prem, Prem bhaiya? I'm back – where are you? Prem?

Prem *enters.*

Lalloo   Bhaiya – you'll never believe what happened! All the doctors had given up on my mother. She hadn't opened her eyes for days. But I had faith. I just knew – Pooja bhabi was praying for her, so nothing could go wrong. Bhaiya – a miracle happened. The day I arrived, she opened her eyes and smiled. I told my mother she was alive because of my bhabi's prayers. My bhabi, whose hand is on my head for ever. I must go and tell her the good news.

Prem   Lalloo – that hand that blessed us all has been taken away from us for ever.

Scene Four

Rajesh, **Kaka**, **Siddarth**, **Kamla** *and* **Nisha**. *They are grieving in front of a garlanded photograph of* **Pooja**. **Lalloo** *enters followed by* **Prem**. **Lalloo** *sees the photo. He walks to photograph. Bows and cries.* **Rajesh** *tries to comfort him.*

Lalloo   What has happened, Rajesh bhaiya? What has happened, Kaka ji? She gave her life so that my mother could be saved. Her blessings saved my mother, but she is gone. Rajesh bhaiya – why has God taken her? Tell me – why has he called such a good and kind person? Answer me, bhaiya!

Kaka   Lalloo – your Pooja bhabi was the epitome of love and piety. God needs good people as well.

Lalloo   What about our little Munna? Doesn't he deserve his mother's love? What's going to happen to him, bhaiya? What's going to happen to him?

Nisha *is humming* **Munna** *to sleep.*

Kaka   Nisha, go and put Munna in his bed.

Nisha   Yes, Papa. (*She leaves.*)

Prof   Bechara. He thinks Nisha's lap is his own mother's.

Kaka   Poor Pooja – she had so much love and affection to give, but as fate would have it, she couldn't give it to her own child . . .

Prem   Bhabi was such a wonderful person. Kaka – how will we live without her?

Rajesh   Prem – Haunsla Rakho. Mummy is upset. (**Kamla** *sobs.*) Come on, Mummy – you need to rest. Let me take you to your room.

They exit. **Arun** *and* **Bhagwanti** *enter.*

Prof   Poor Rajesh. We all miss Pooja, but just think what he must be going through. I've lost a daughter, but he has lost his whole life.

Arun   He is comforting everyone – but what comfort can we offer him?

Kaka   Yes, what can anyone say?

Arun   The strange thing about life is that it doesn't stop.

Kaka   You are right. No matter what tragedy occurs, you still have to face tomorrow.

Arun   Han – when my sister and your brother were killed, straight away we had to put our grief aside and think about the boys . . .

Bhagwanti   Bhai Sahib – Rajesh should remarry.

Arun   Bhagwanti!

Kaka   Pooja passed away only a week ago. It's far too soon to think about that.

Bhagwanti   The sooner the better. Sweetie is still available and willing to marry him. If he'd married her in the first place, none of this would have happened.

Arun   Bhagwanti – keep quiet.

Bhagwanti   You stay out of it – I'm thinking of Rajesh. I've already talked to Sweetie. She's willing – on one condition: she would need an ayah to look after Munna.

Lalloo   An ayah to look after our little Munna?

Bhagwanti   Who are you to give your opinion? He's getting too big for his boots. Everyone has ayahs these days – what's the problem?

Lalloo   Prem bhaiya – please don't agree to this. Munna is our only reminder of Pooja bhabi. You can't hand him over to an ayah.

Bhagwanti   This servant – who does he think he is?

Arun   Lalloo is right, Bhagwanti. Your niece hasn't an ounce of maternal love to give to anyone. She is too selfish. I can't imagine her loving her own children, let alone someone else's.

Bhagwanti   What bakwas! You are criticising my niece for no rhyme or reason. Who is willing to become a stepmother these days? You tell me! Which parents would offer their daughter to Rajesh? Ask the professor – would you be willing to marry Nisha to Rajesh?

Arun   Bhagwanti – will you shut up! You've said enough.

Bhagwanti   Don't you dare lecture me! Keep your lectures for your students. Kaka, for once you should listen to me: Rajesh should marry Sweetie and get an ayah. People make such a fuss about children. Munna will grow up. He won't know the difference between a mother and an ayah . . .

Arun *slaps her.*

Arun   It is this sour nature of yours that has kept us childless all our lives!

She exits sobbing.

Arun   I'm so sorry – so very, very sorry, everyone.

He exits. Silence.

Kaka   Bhagwanti gets carried away sometimes. We are all upset . . .

Prem   This time she has gone too far. Talking about marriage, when bhaiya is still mourning Pooja bhabi . . .

Prof   Well, Prem – hard as it is for me to say this, Kamla and I would not want Rajesh to pine for Pooja all his life. Bhagwanti had a point – he should remarry sooner or later, and why not while Munna is still a baby?

Kaka   Siddarth – who would be willing to be a stepmother?

Rajesh *enters.*

Prof   Every stepmother is not hard-hearted, Kailash
Nath . . .

Rajesh   Auntie has taken a sedative. Perhaps now she will
get some rest.

Prof   Bless you, beta. Now, Rajesh – I am Pooja's father. I
know what you are going through, but you must think about
Munna's future. He needs a mother.

Rajesh   Papa – Pooja's memory is enough for Munna and
me.

Prof   You will still have that memory, but you must think
practically. Today we are all here: me, Kamla, your Kaka –
but we won't be here for ever. You need a companion at
every stage of life. It's not easy to bring up a child. It's a big
responsibility, Rajesh.

Rajesh   Who would take a child who is not theirs into
their heart?

Prof   I agree – you need someone who would be like
Munna's own mother. Will you accept Nisha? Since Pooja
died, Munna has been with Nisha day and night. She is his
aunt – Bhagwanti Behn is right. Only she can take her
sister's place as his mother.

Kaka   Siddarth – are you sure?

Prof   I would be more than happy and I know Kamla
would agree with me.

Kaka   Prem – what do you think?

Prem   Rajesh bhaiya, you should accept the proposal.

Lalloo   Prem bhaiya?

Kaka   Rajesh – what do you think? It's a good solution.

Rajesh   You must first ask Nisha.

Prof   We will ask her. If she agrees, we will have a grand wedding – it will bring a new lease of life to this house.

Nisha *enters.*

Nisha   Munna is asleep now.

Prof   Good. Nisha beti – I have something important to ask you. I know it is early days and we are still grieving for your sister, but how would you feel about coming into this house as a daughter-in-law?

Nisha *says nothing, but thinking they mean for her to marry* **Prem***, she is clearly delighted.*

Prof   In Pooja's absence, only you can make this house blossom again. What do you say, Nisha?

Nisha   Whatever you feel is right, Papa.

Prof   Kailash Nath – consult the Pandit straight away for an auspicious date.

Kaka   You have made us all very happy, Nisha.

Prem *exits.*

Prof   Kailash – tomorrow, we'll leave and start making preparations. And may I suggest that we take Munna with us? He is so used to Nisha now – it will upset him to be without her. After all, it's only until the wedding day.

Kaka   Of course. Chalo.

They all exit.

Scene Five

Back at **Nisha***'s house. It is night – there is quiet. It is the night before the Mehndi celebration.*

Kamla *enters with* **Munna***.*

Kamla   Nisha! Nisha!

Nisha (*entering*)   Yes, Mummy?

Kamla   Come here, darling.

Nisha   Is he asleep?

Kamla   Yes. So much has happened in his short life and he is so innocent. He has no idea . . .

Nisha   He never knew didi to miss her.

Kamla   And now that you are entering the house, he'll never have to miss her.

Nisha   Han.

Kamla   You are happy, aren't you, darling?

Nisha   Of course I am. Why shouldn't I be?

Kamla   These are not ideal cirmcumstances in which to get married, but your papa and I still want what is best for you.

Nisha   Mama – I'm very happy.

Kamla   You are a good girl. Your didi is watching and knows that Munna will be well cared for by you.

Nisha   I love him as if he were mine.

Kamla   You'll have your own children as well. Brothers and sisters for Munna.

Nisha   Han.

Kamla   I'm going to sleep now, darling. Tomorrow is a very big day. Your Mehndi is the first of so many celebrations. I'm going to lose another daughter . . .

She cries. **Nisha** *embraces her.*

Nisha   Come on, Mummy. You go to bed now.

Kamla   You too have an early night.

Nisha   Han – good night, Mummy.

She sings to **Munna**.

> Fortune gives, but fortune takes,
> My happiness aches with grieving,
> But we must look, for all our sakes,
> At what the strength of love is achieving.
>
> Fortune smiles, but fortune frowns,
> This fortune drowns my sorrow.
> From funeral white, to wedding gowns
> I'll marry my Prem tomorrow.
>
> Poor little baby so unaware
> Of why we cry this way.
> And my poor didi, she won't be there
> To share my happiest day.

She exits with **Munna**.

Scene Six

Mehndi celebration in **Nisha**'s *House.*

Song: 'Mother, Oh Mother'

Nisha and Girls   Mother, oh Mother
There in the skies
A jet-black crow is gliding.
Mother, oh Mother
See how it flies
Above where the groom is riding.
Love is a sunrise, dark flies away,
Love is like the dawn today.
Mother, oh Mother
Now up above
There's a dove with snow-white
    feathers.
There in her breast
A beating like wings
Her heartbeat races and sings.

Come on now, let's dance,
Come on, take a chance.
Come on, it's time for a party.
Come on now, let's dance,
Come on, take a chance.
Come on, it's time for a party.

Nisha *is with two of her friends upstairs in the bedroom (***Rita** *and* **Radha***). There is a party downstairs. This is a split stage, as this whole scene is continuous.*

Kamla *and the* **Professor** *are downstairs. The doorbell rings. The* **Professor** *answers the door.* **Kaka** *and* **Rajesh** *enter.*

Prof/Kamla   Namaste, Kailash/Namaste, Rajesh.

Kaka   Namaste.

Prof   Come in, come in . . .

Kaka   How are the preparations going?

Prof   Can't you hear the girls singing upstairs?

Kaka   I've got the sample of the wedding invitation.

Prof   Thank you for picking it up for me.

Rajesh   It was no problem, Papa – it was on our way.

Kamla   I'll get Nisha to have a look at it . . .

She calls upstairs.

Kamla   Radha!

Radha *comes downstairs.*

Kamla   Ask Nisha if she likes the invitation.

Radha   OK, Auntie.

Rajesh   Where's Munna?

Prof   He's in the garden with one of Nisha's friends. Go and see him. Not long to wait now till he's back in your home.

Rajesh   I wanted to speak to Nisha.

Kamla   She'll be down soon.

Rajesh *goes into garden.*
Prof, **Kamla**, **Kaka** *sit and chat.*
Focus shifts upstairs.

Radha   Nisha – look what I've got in my hand.

Nisha   What?

Radha   The wedding card – for your approval.

Rita   Read it – read it out loud!

Radha   'With God's Grace, our daughter Nisha is to be married to Rajesh. Please grace our wedding celebrations by attending with your family . . .'

Nisha   What are you doing? Read it properly!

Radha   I am. It says, 'With God's Grace, our daughter Nisha is to be married to Rajesh. Please grace our wedding celebrations by attending with your family and joining us in wishing the bride and bridegroom a prosperous life.'

Nisha   Show it to me . . .

Radha   What's the problem?

Nisha *reads the invitation. She runs downstairs and bumps into* **Kaka**.

Nisha   Kaka – have you seen Mummy? I need to talk to her.

Kaka   I think she is busy with some guests.

Nisha   I need to see her . . .

Kaka   Nisha – I am eternally grateful to you for agreeing to marry Rajesh. Look in the garden – see how happy he is? You have given two lost souls a new lease of life. How can I ever thank you?

Nisha *looks out to garden. She faints.* **Kamla** *runs over.*

Prof   Nisha – Nisha beti! – What's happened?

Kaka   She suddenly fainted!

Prof   Poor thing. She's completely worn out with all the excitement and celebrations. Take her upstairs. Let her lie down for a while. Kamla!

Kamla   What has happened?

Kaka   She just fainted. Kamla – don't you think we should call a doctor?

Prof   No, darling. Let her rest and then we'll see. I'm sure it's just the commotion.

They exit.

Kaka   It's all happened so quickly – it's a lot for Nisha to take on . . .

Prof   Kailash – Nisha is very happy. She is just overexcited.

Rajesh *returns with* **Munna**.

Rajesh   Has Nisha come down yet?

Prof   Actually, she's resting now, Rajesh – she's worn out.

Rajesh   Oh – I hope everything is all right.

Prof   Of course, beta. It's just the excitement that has overtired her.

Rajesh   Well, I did want to speak to her, but I'll leave her a note then if I may?

Prof   Of course.

Rajesh *gives* **Munna** *to the* **Professor**. *He takes a pen and paper out of his pocket and steps aside to write his note.*

Kaka   Who could have expected so much happiness out of such misfortune?

Prof   Han – we are very lucky. We must celebrate in the same way we did when Pooja and Rajesh got married. No expense spared. Nisha must not feel that she is second best.

Kamla   She's all right now.

Prof   I told you she would be.

Kamla   Let me take Munna. He should also be having his afternoon sleep now.

She exits with **Munna**.

Rajesh   Papa – will you give this to Nisha for me? (*Hands him letter.*)

Prof   Certainly, beta.

Kaka   OK then – we must go and leave you to it.

Prof   Rajesh – please – between now and the wedding, feel free to come over at any time when you want to see Munna.

Rajesh   Thank you, Papa.

They exit.

Scene Seven

Nisha's *bedroom.* **Professor** *comes quietly into room.*

Prof   Nisha, beti – are you all right?

Nisha   Yes, Papa.

Prof   You are overexcited, aren't you?

Nisha   Yes.

Prof   We are so proud of what you are doing, Nisha.

Nisha   Papa?

Prof   Yes, beti?

Nisha   . . . Nothing. I think I need to rest . . .

Prof   Yes – you rest. I just came to give you this letter that Rajesh has left for you.

He exits. **Nisha** *opens letter.* **Rajesh***'s voice is heard as she reads it.*

Rajesh   'Nisha, I will always be indebted to you for this step that you have taken for Munna and me. Everyone else is also delighted. But I also know that every young woman has her own dreams and desires. So please, if you have any doubt in your heart about what you are about to do, then I would ask you to share it with me now, because your happiness is more important to me than anything else. Yours, Rajesh.'

Nisha *picks up phone. Dials. Another phone rings on the other side of the stage.* **Prem** *comes on and picks it up.*

Prem   Hello. Who is it?

Song: 'Now Love's a Memory'

Nisha   Hey hey hey
Hey hey hey
Hey hey hey
Hey hey hey.

Now love's a memoy, I'll wipe it from my heart.
The things I'd hoped to be are gone before they
      start.

Hey hey hey.

Prem   We carry on through life, as duty says we must.
The gods choose man and wife,
We marry with their trust.
I bow my head to you, won't show my breaking
      heart
So proud our love was true, but now we have to
      part.

Scene Eight

Nisha's *house. Chat and general atmosphere. A small wedding band sets the wedding scene.* **Kamla**, **Arun**, **Bhagwanti**, **Kaka**, **Professor**, **Lalloo**, **Rajesh**, **Prem**, **Female Servant** – *all downstairs.* **Nisha** *is upstairs writing a letter.*

Prof   Well, Rajesh – you will be spared the pranks this time. You are marrying the gang leader.

Prem   Bhaiya – we still better be on our guard. Knowing Nisha, she's probably delegated her position to someone else.

Rajesh   We'll make sure that you and Lalloo watch my shoes when I take them off for the ceremony.

Rajesh *goes and joins others.* **Female Servant** *goes upstairs to* **Nisha**. **Nisha** *indicates to her to call* **Lalloo**. *In the meantime:*

Lalloo   Bhaiya – your wide smile and laughter doesn't fool me.

Prem   Lalloo, you promised not to say anything.

Lalloo   Yes – you have sworn me to secrecy, but this is not right . . .

Prem *moves away.*

Lalloo (*to his Krishna*)   'Dear Lord, what a situation we are in! I have given my promise to Prem Bhaiya – my lips are sealed, but you are not bound by any such promise. Please, Lord, perform a miracle today, so that people's faith in you is renewed and they believe in you more and more. Please, God . . . please.'

Servant   Nisha ji is wanting you.

Lalloo   Where is she?

Servant   Upstairs in her bedroom.

He goes up.

Lalloo   You called for me?

Nisha   Han, Lalloo – I want you to do something for me. Give this to Prem.

She hands him the necklace and a letter wrapped up in a handkerchief.

Lalloo   Nisha ji . . .

Nisha   Lalloo – don't say anything.

He takes the packet and goes downstairs. On his way he encounters **Kaka**.

Kaka   What are you doing upstairs?

Lalloo   Nisha ji had called me . . .

Kaka   Everything all right?

Lalloo   Han.

Kaka   Oh, Lalloo – what a great day! First it was our fortune to have Pooja come into our home and now Nisha is doing this for us. Truly – we are blessed.

Lalloo   Han. Aah . . . Kaka?

Kaka   Yes, Lalloo?

Lalloo   What time is the ceremony?

Kaka   Any time now.

Lalloo   Good.

Prof   Kailash Nath!

Kaka   Excuse me, Lalloo.

Lalloo   Han. 'Oh Krishna ji – what now? It is nearly doomsday . . .'

Rajesh *approaches.*

Rajesh   Who are you talking to, Lalloo?

Lalloo   God.

Rajesh   All set, then?

Lalloo   Han, bhaiya.

Rajesh   Remember – keep an eye on my shoes.

Lalloo   Han, bhaiya.

Rajesh   What's that you've got there?

Lalloo   Aah – nothing, nothing, bhaiya . . .

Lalloo *accidentally drops the package.* **Rajesh** *picks it up.*

Lalloo   Oh no!

Rajesh   What is this? – my mother's necklace? What's going on, Lalloo?

Lalloo   I . . . I promised Prem Bhaiya. I am not allowed to say anything . . .

Rajesh *opens and reads the letter.*

Nisha's voice   'Prem, Pooja sealed our bond of love with your mother's necklace. She wanted to see her younger sister-in-law wear it, so I am returning it to you to give to your future wife. Nisha.'

Prem *approaches.*

Lalloo (*to his Krishna charm*)   Thank you, Lord, for choosing me as your messenger.

Rajesh   Prem – what is all this?

Rajesh *goes to stairs and calls.*

Rajesh   Nisha – could you come downstairs please?

Nisha *enters. All gather round.*

Rajesh   What is this, Nisha?

Rajesh (*addresses the large photograph of* **Pooja** *on the wall*) Look, Pooja – what these two were about to do? Can you imagine if we had gone through with this wedding?

Kaka   What's happened?

Rajesh   Read this, Kaka.

Kaka *reads the letter, then* **Professor***, then* **Kamla***, who has* **Munna***.*

Rajesh   What an injustice we would have committed had this gone ahead! Kaka – look at your beloved Prem. He used to confide in me the smallest things and now he has kept such a big thing hidden in his heart. Buried in his laughter and smiles. He has truly treated me like a stranger today.

Prem   Bhaiya . . .

Rajesh   No – what you did was not right. Mummy, after Pooja passed away, my one wish was that Moona would not feel the lack of a mother's love. Tell me, Nisha – if you had taken in my son and given him all your love as my brother's wife, would there be any difference between that love and the love you would give him as a stepmother? . . . Answer me, Nisha: why are you silent?

Nisha *cries.*

Rajesh   Pagli – you were going to sacrifice your whole life, your chance of happiness?

Arun   Rajesh beta – we should applaud them. They were only doing what they felt was their duty.

Rajesh   Well, I too have a duty. Pooja knew something none of us knew and she was trying to tell us that at the hospital. I must now fulfil her wishes. Pooja – the truth is that it is my fault. I blame myself for not understanding what you were trying to say in your last moments. Papa – I have one request. Please give Nisha's hand in marriage to Prem.

Prof   Kailash Nath – I must have done some good deeds in my previous life to deserve such a son-in-law as Rajesh. I

am truly blessed. Well, we are prepared for a wedding, so –
what are we waiting for?

Hugs and kisses all round.
Prem *and* **Nisha** *go to touch* **Rajesh**'s *feet.*

Bhagwanti   Welcome, Nisha. Both families are so well
suited. My niece, Sweetie, has broken off yet another
engagement. How could I ever have imagined that she
could fit into this home?

Arun   Darling – we all make mistakes. And I too have a
confession to make . . . It was me that introduced Pooja into
this family!

Bhagwanti   You rascal!

They all laugh.

Song: 'Dikthana'

All   Dikthana, Dikthana, Dikthana, Dik Dikthana,
          Dikthana, Dikthana
          Dikthana, Dikthana, Dikthana, Oh
          Dikthana, Dikthana, Dikthana

Lalloo   I am love's servant for Prem and Nisha.

All   Dikthana, Dikthana, Dikthana, Dik
          Dikthana, Dikthana, Dikthana
          Dikthana, Dikthana, Dikthana, Oh
          Dikthana, Dikthana, Dikthana

Rajesh   With so much joy, their day is filled.
          You can't destroy what fate has willed.
          A different wedding,
          But a happy ending for Prem and Nisha.

All   Dikthana, Dikthana, Dikthana, Dik
          Dikthana, Dikthana, Dikthana
          Dikthana, Dikthana, Dikthana, Oh
          Dikthana, Dikthana, Dikthana

Repeat.

Blackout.